Glorious Mysteries

Photo Rosary

Contents

Opening Prayers

Sign of the Cross
Apostle's Creed
prayers for the pope
Our Father
Three Hail Marys
Glory Be

First Glorious Mystery

The Resurrection

Our Father

Hail Mary

Hail Mary

Hail Mary

Hail Mary

10
Hail Mary

Hail Mary

Hail Mary

Hail Mary

Hail Mary

Hail Mary

Glory Be

IHS
Oh, My Jesus

Second Glorious Mystery

The Ascension

Our Father

Hail Mary

Hail Mary

Hail Mary

Hail Mary

Hail Mary

V
iri galilei quid
admiramini
aspicientes in
celum alleluya queadmo
dum vidistis eum ascenden
tem in celum ita veniet al
leluya allia alleluya. ps.
O
mnes gentes plaudite
Hail Mary

26
Hail Mary

Hail Mary

Hail Mary

Hail Mary

Glory Be

Oh, My Jesus

Third Glorious Mystery

The Descent of the Holy Spirit

Our Father

Hail Mary

Hail Mary

Hail Mary

Hail Mary

Hail Mary

Hail Mary

40
Hail Mary

Hail Mary

Hail Mary

Hail Mary

Glory Be

Oh, My Jesus

Fourth Glorious Mystery

The Assumption

Our Father

Hail Mary

Hail Mary

Hail Mary

Hail Mary

Hail Mary

Hail Mary

Hail Mary

Hail Mary

Hail Mary

Hail Mary

Glory Be

Oh, My Jesus

Fifth Glorious Mystery

The Coronation

Our Father

Hail Mary

Hail Mary

Hail Mary

Hail Mary

Hail Mary

Hail Mary

Hail Mary

Hail Mary

Hail Mary

Hail Mary

Glory Be

IHS
Oh, My Jesus

Hail Holy Queen

Made in the USA
Coppell, TX
16 June 2023